EBONY ESSENCE

A COLORING BOOK FOR GROWN UPS CELEBRATING BLACK WOMEN AND GIRLS

By Dr. LaShawnda Lindsay-Dennis,
The Crafty Ph.D.

Ananse Design Essentials

Copyright © 2017 LaShawnda Lindsay-Dennis, Ph.D.

All rights reserved. This book or any portion thereof may not be reproduced or used in any manner whatsoever without the express written permission of the publisher except for the use of brief quotations in a book review.

ISBN-13: 978-1979618427
ISBN-10: 1979618429

Book design by Megan Cassidy
Cover design, texts, and illustrations:
Copyright © 2017 LaShawnda Lindsay-Dennis, Ph.D.

First Printing November 2017
Printed by CreateSpace

Published by Ananse Design Essentials

Learn More: AnanseDesignEssentials.com

To my Granny,
Annie Will Butler.

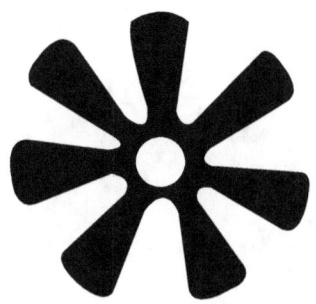

For TeTe's baby, Robyn.
TeTe did not leave you.

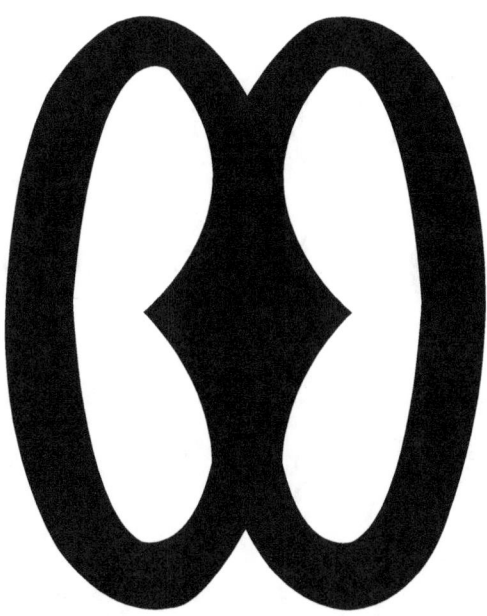

hope (v). / hōp /
1. to cherish a desire with anticipation :to want something to happen or be true
2. to desire with expectation of obtainment or fulfillment
3. to expect with confidence

These definitions of hope embody the impetus for the creation of images in this coloring book. My **H.O.P.E.** is that this coloring book provides a way for you to **H**eal **O**utwardly **P**rivate **E**motions. This work has grown out of intense, innate need to express things that ail and anchor my soul. For me, artistic expression—drawing, painting, crafting, making, and other artisan work—provides a space for me to escape from the stress of everyday life and make a positive, meaningful contribution to my aesthetic environment and to those of others. This book is a manifestation of these modalities that I use to quiet the ramblings of my heart, mind, body, and soul.

Each figure was carefully crafted and adorned with West African Adinkra symbols meant to give meaning, depth, and breadth to each image. The symbol on this page represents hope. You can learn more about each of the symbols that are embedded in these images at AnanseDesignEssentials.com.

My **H.O.P.E.** is that the images that are on these pages help you to heal, create, and celebrate your inner and outer beauty.

— Dr. LaShawnda Lindsay-Dennis,
The Crafty Ph.D.

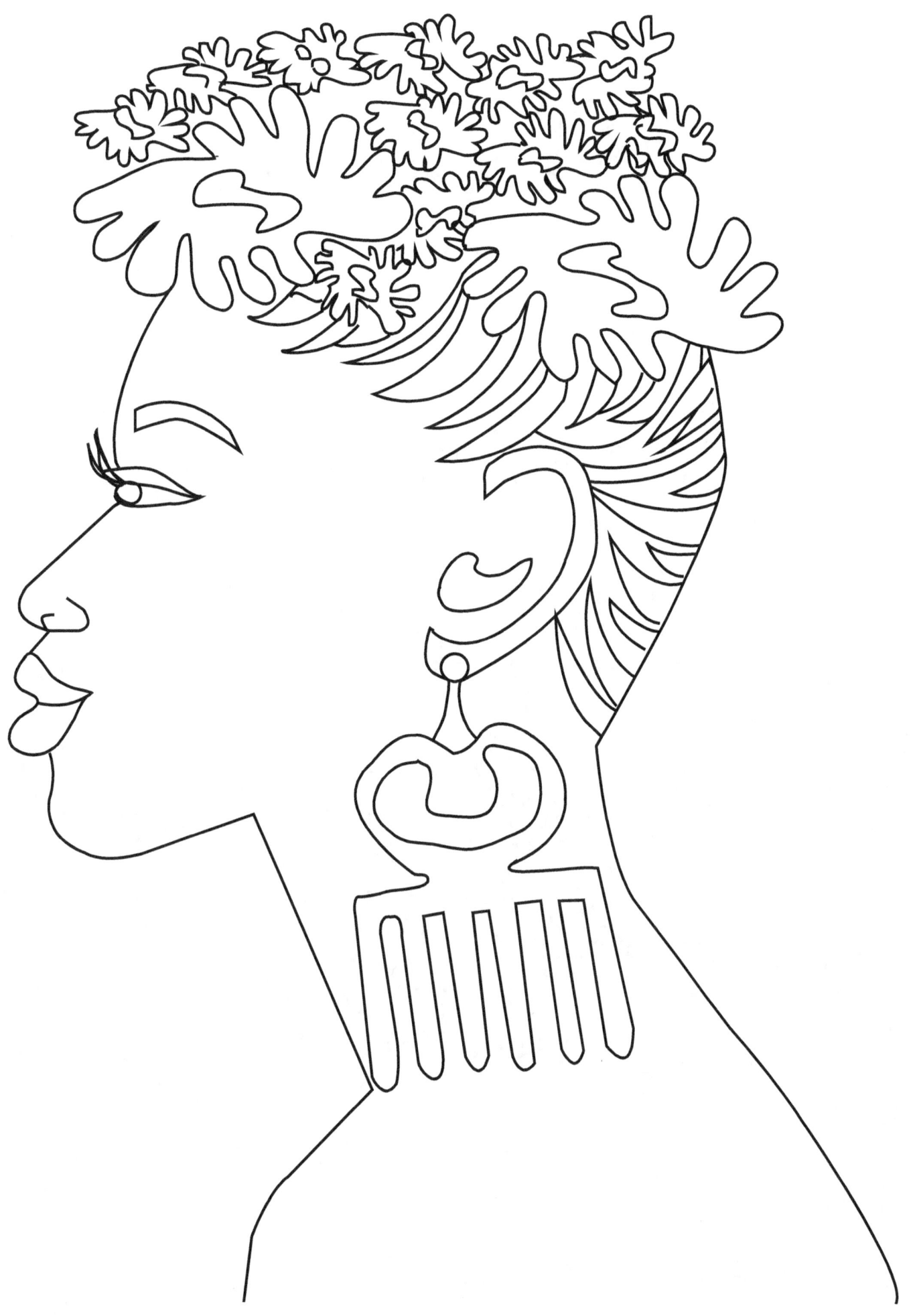

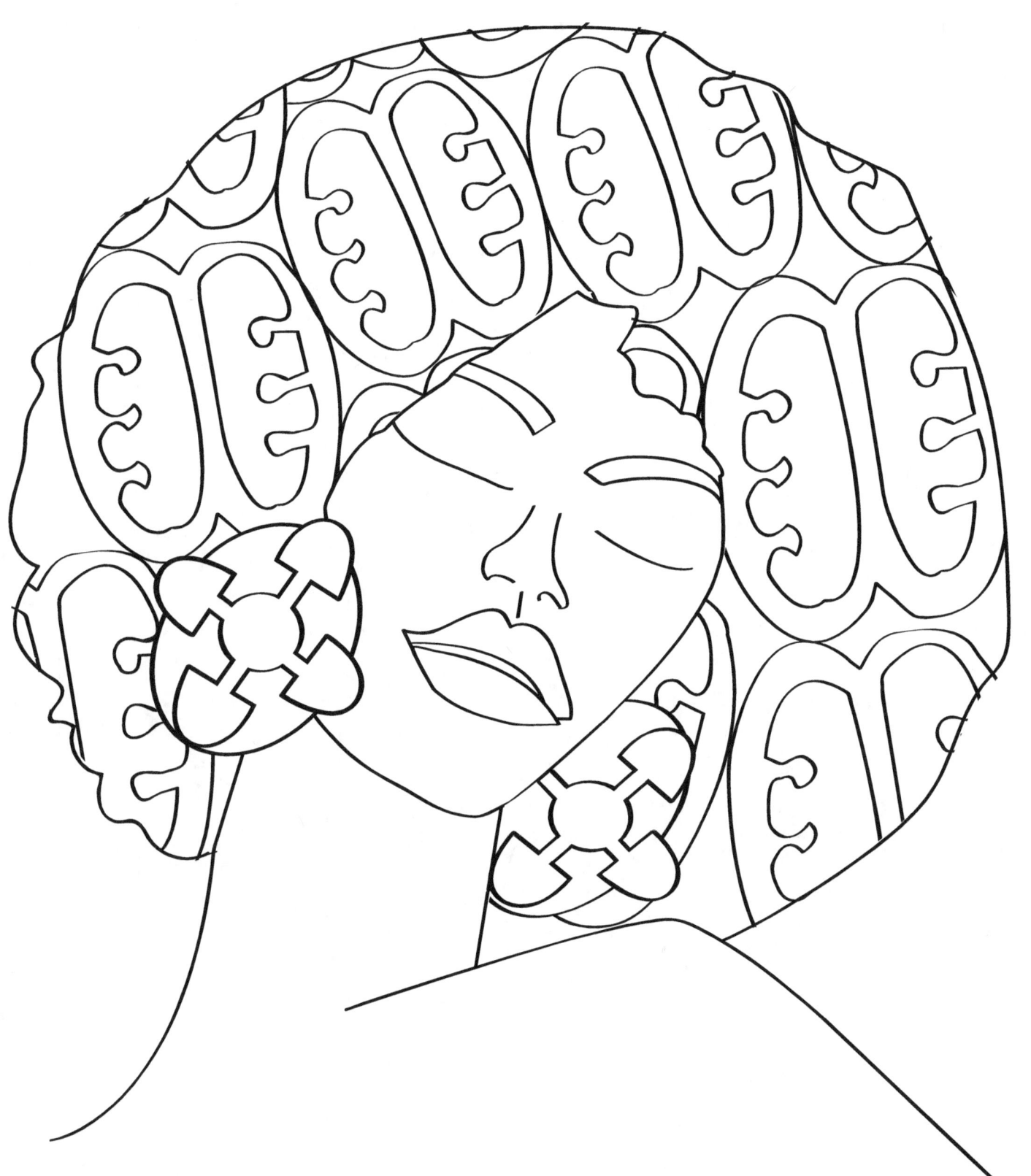

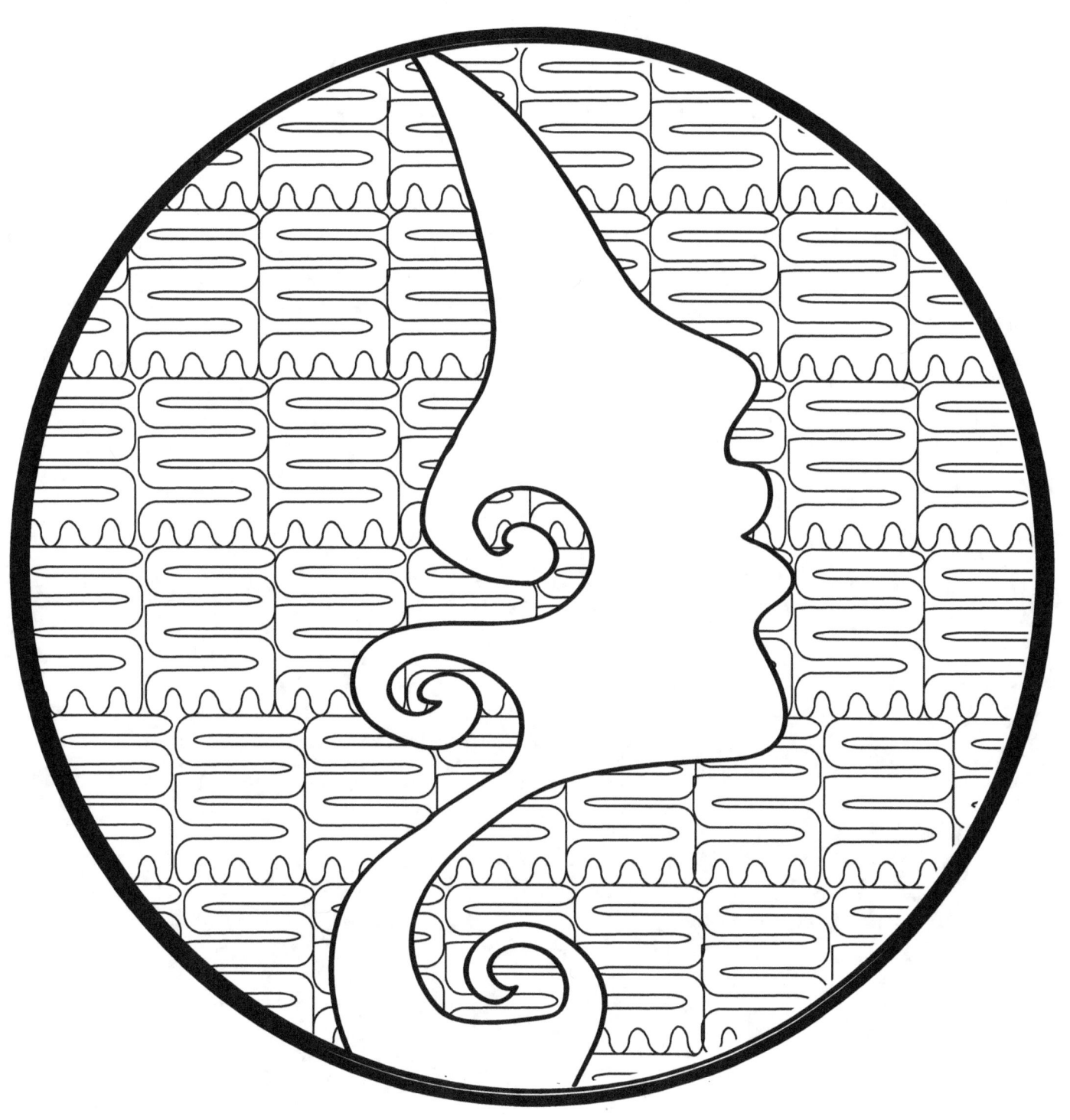

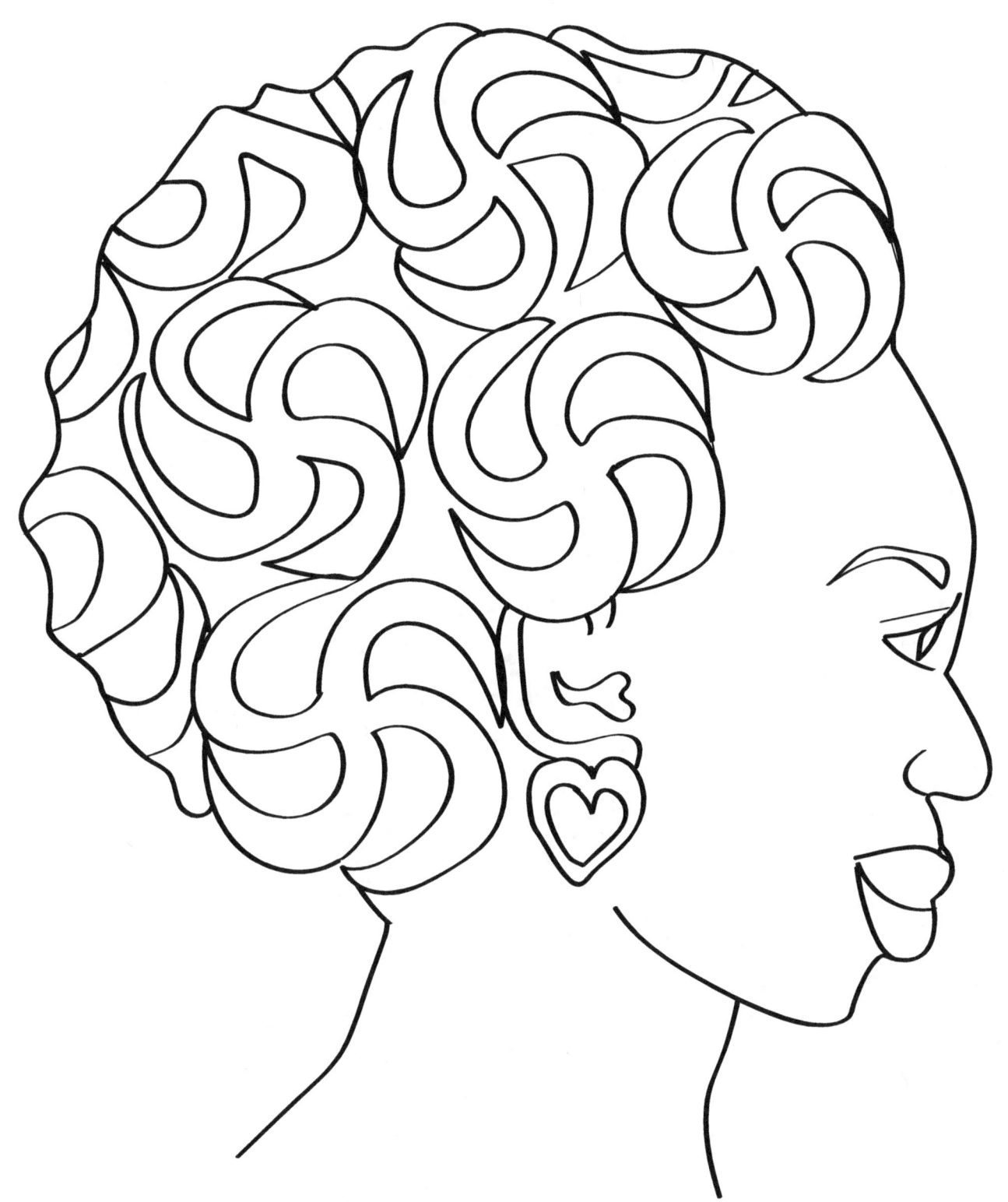

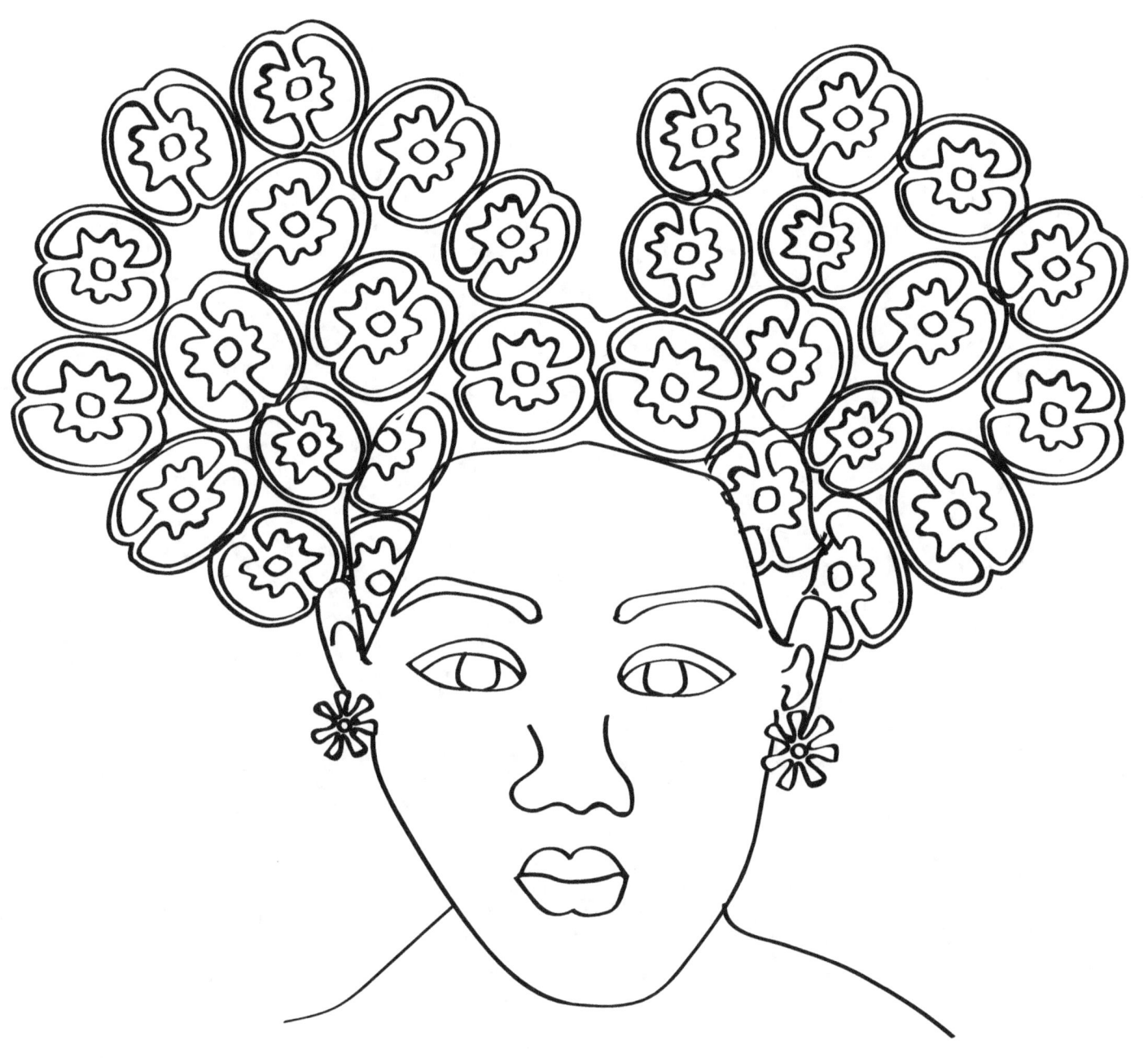

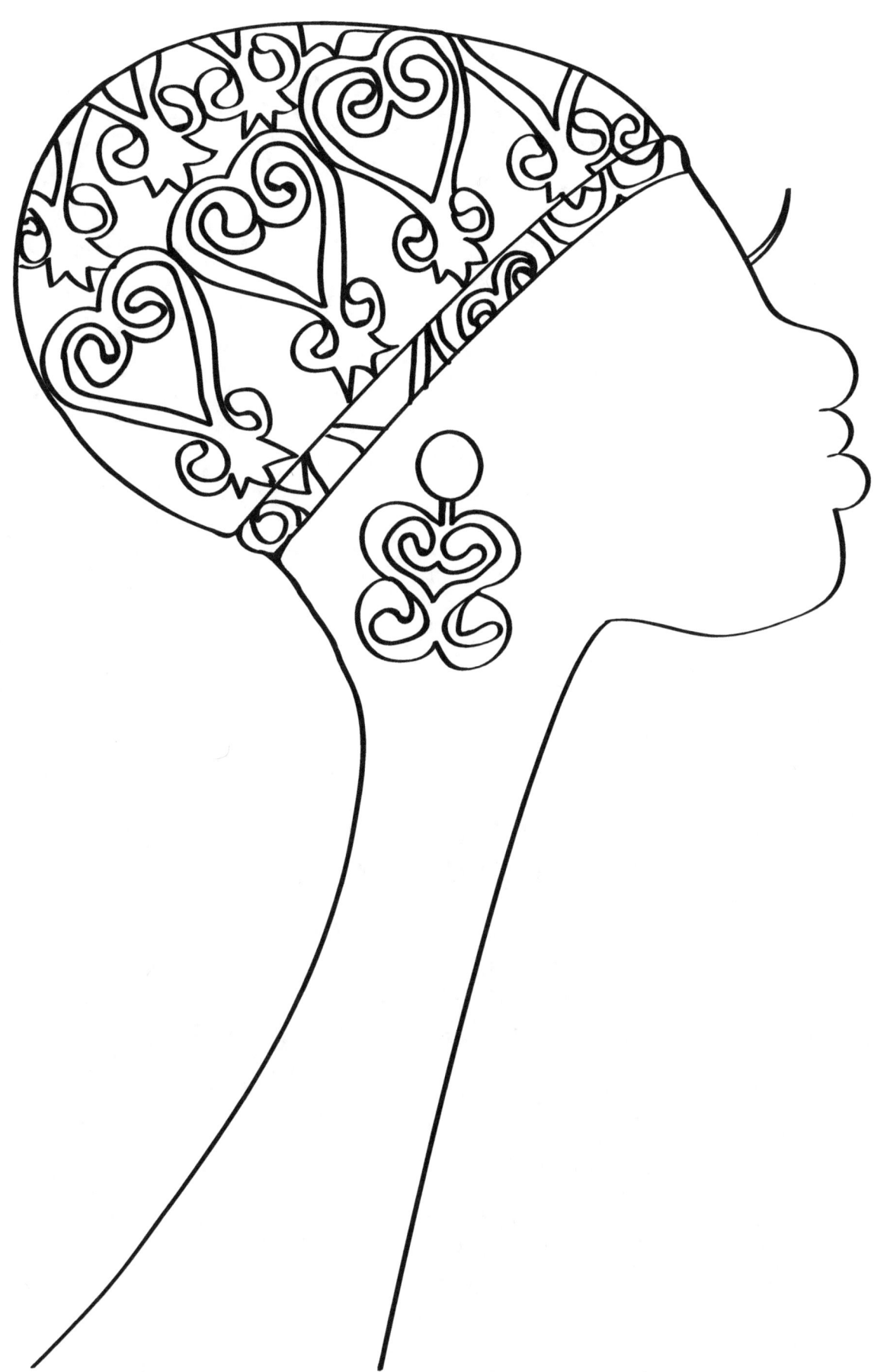

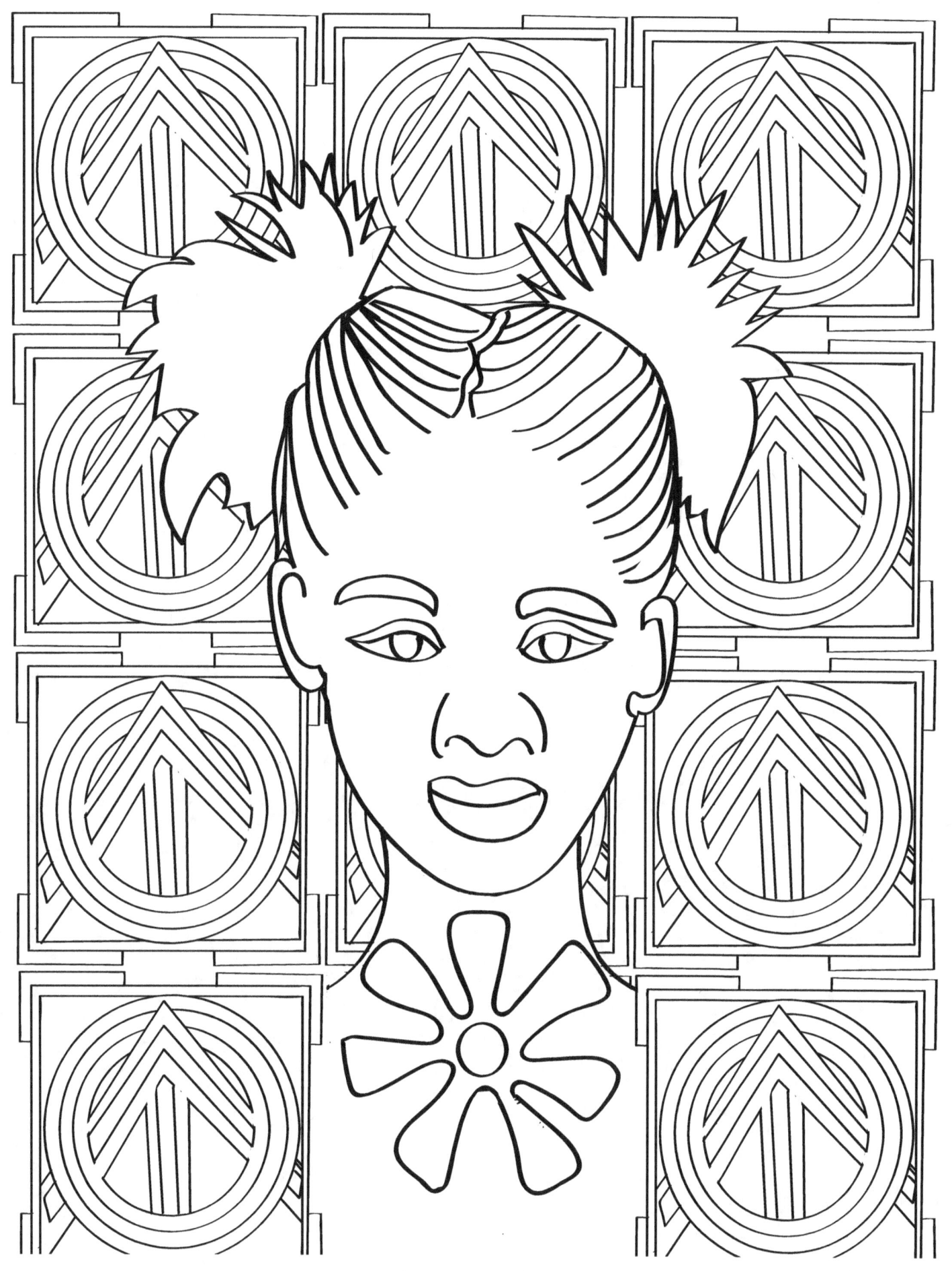

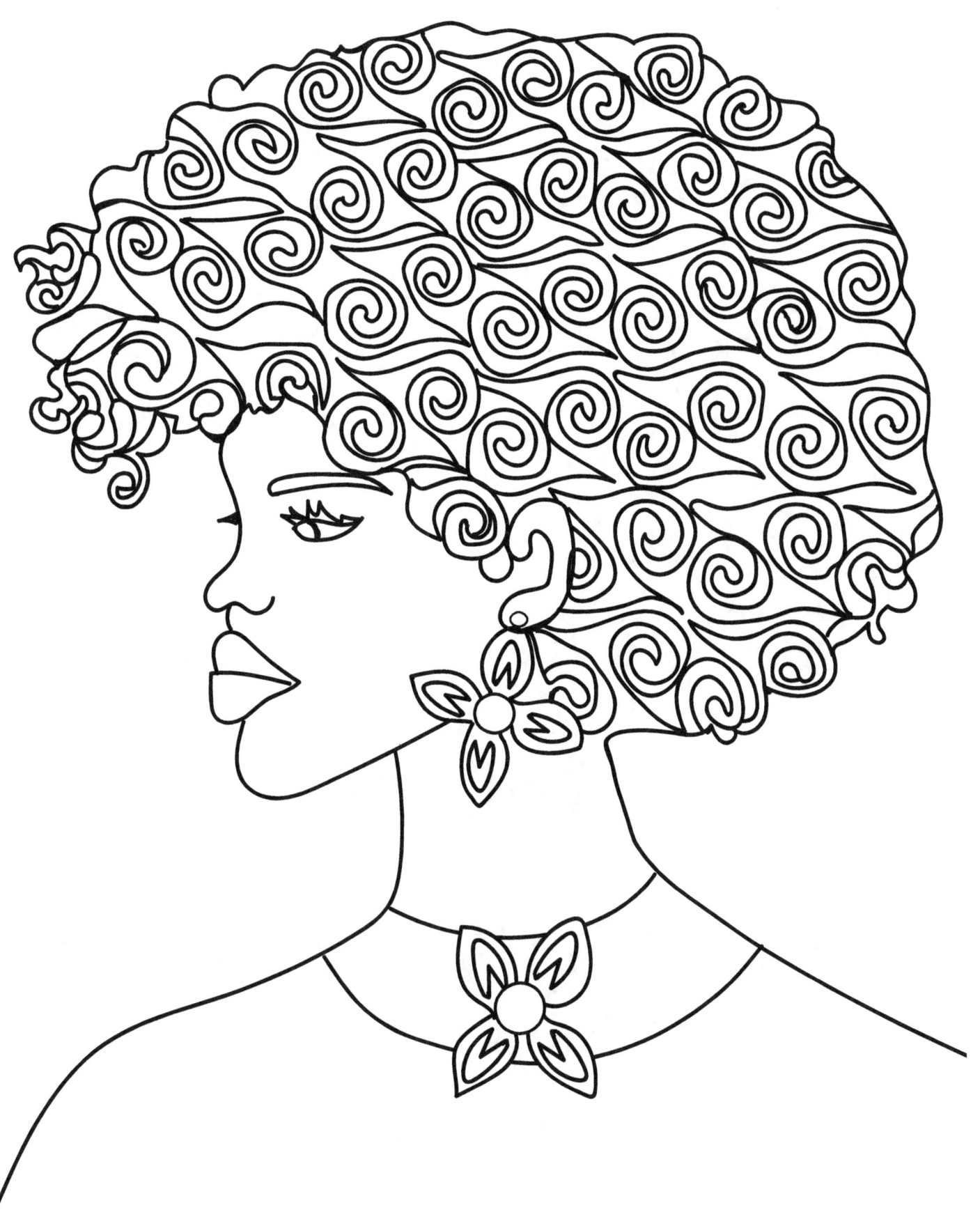

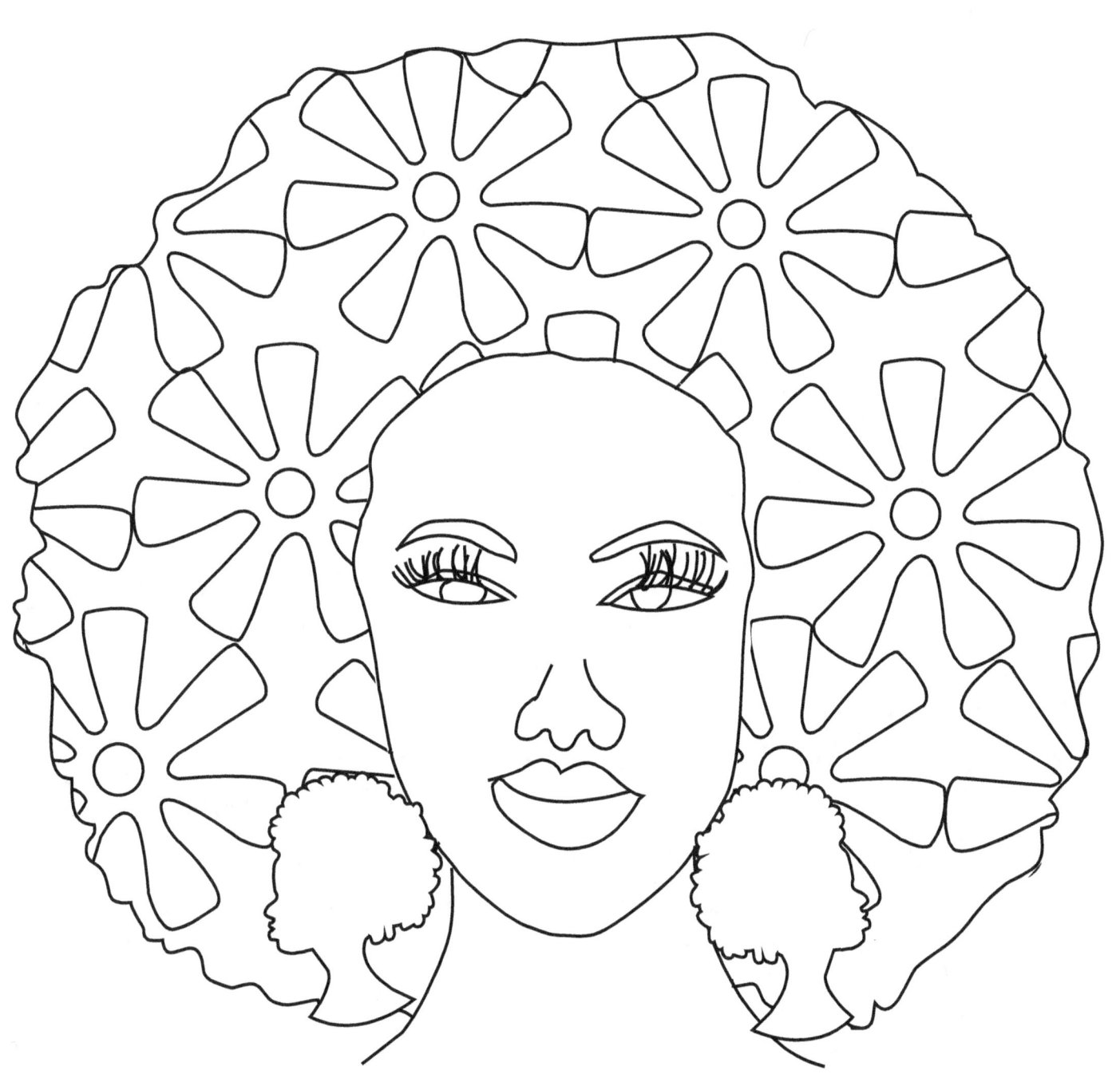

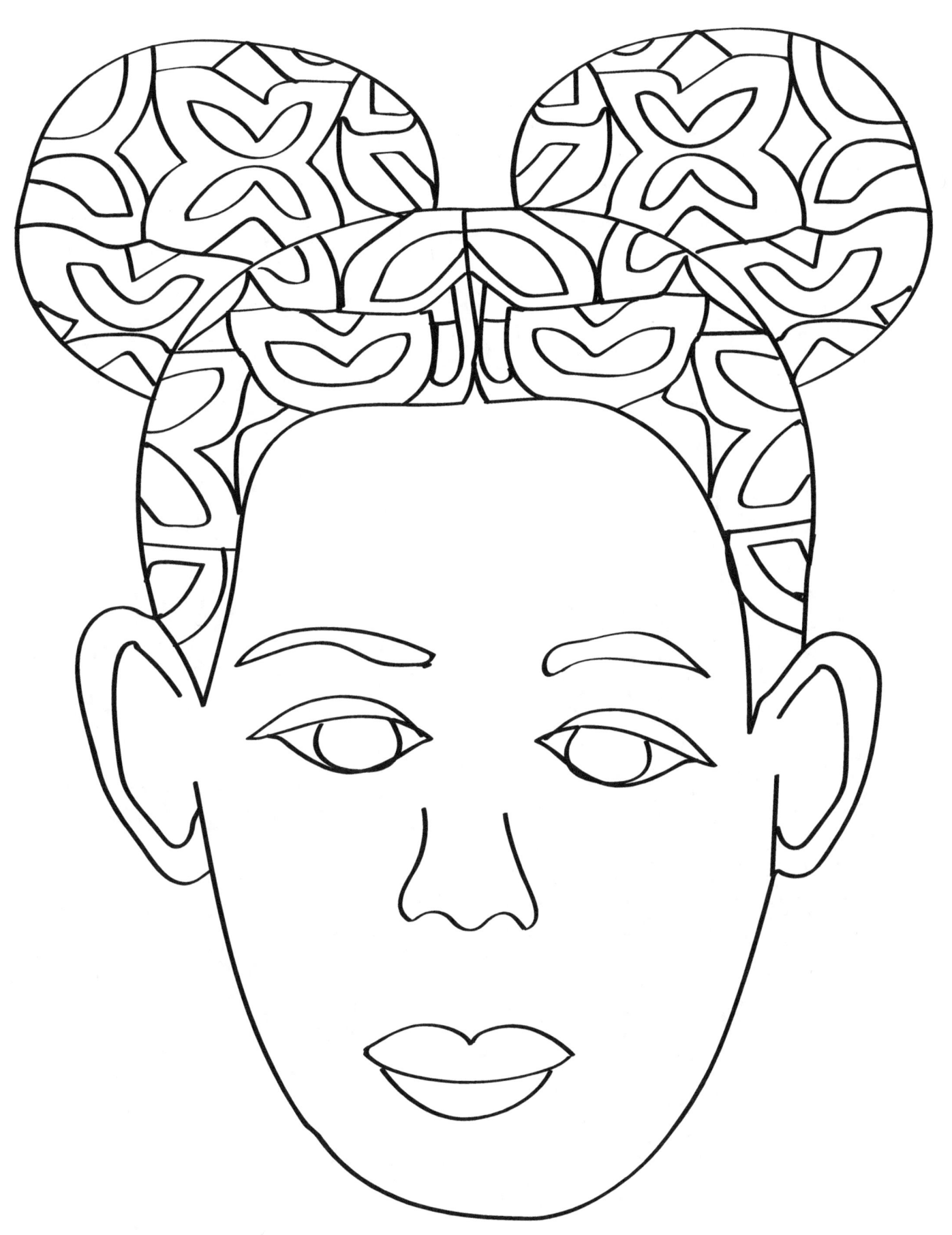

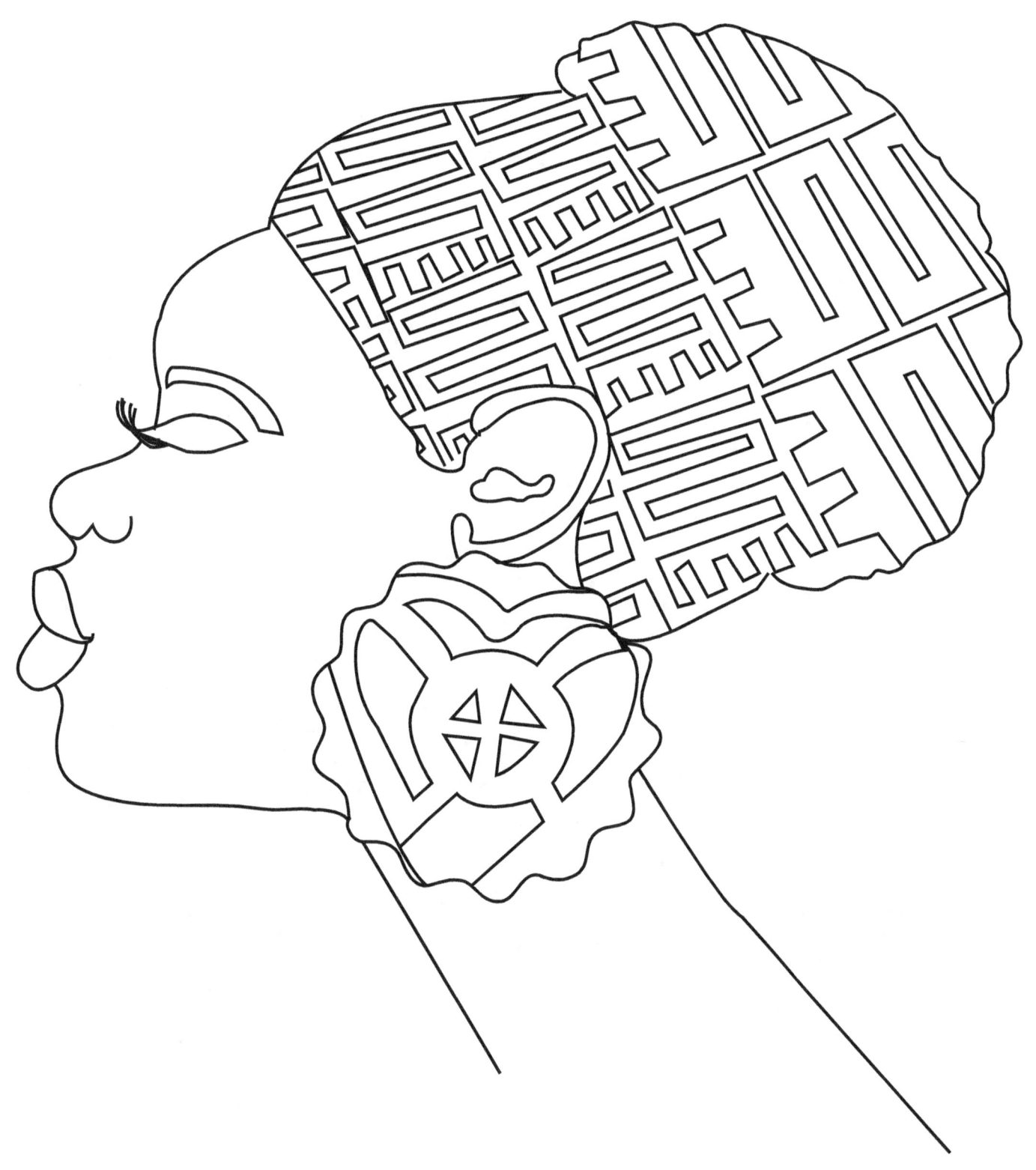

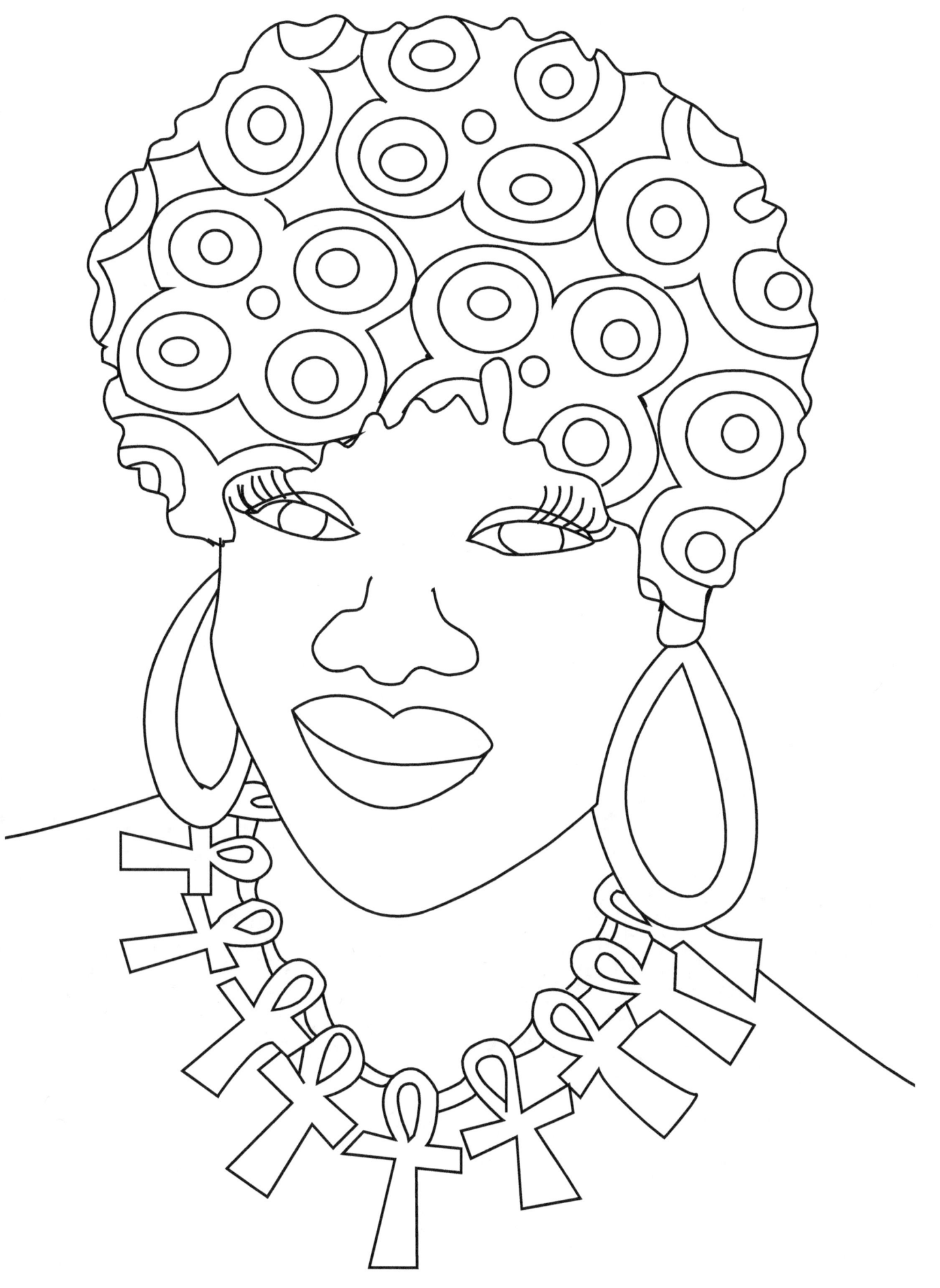

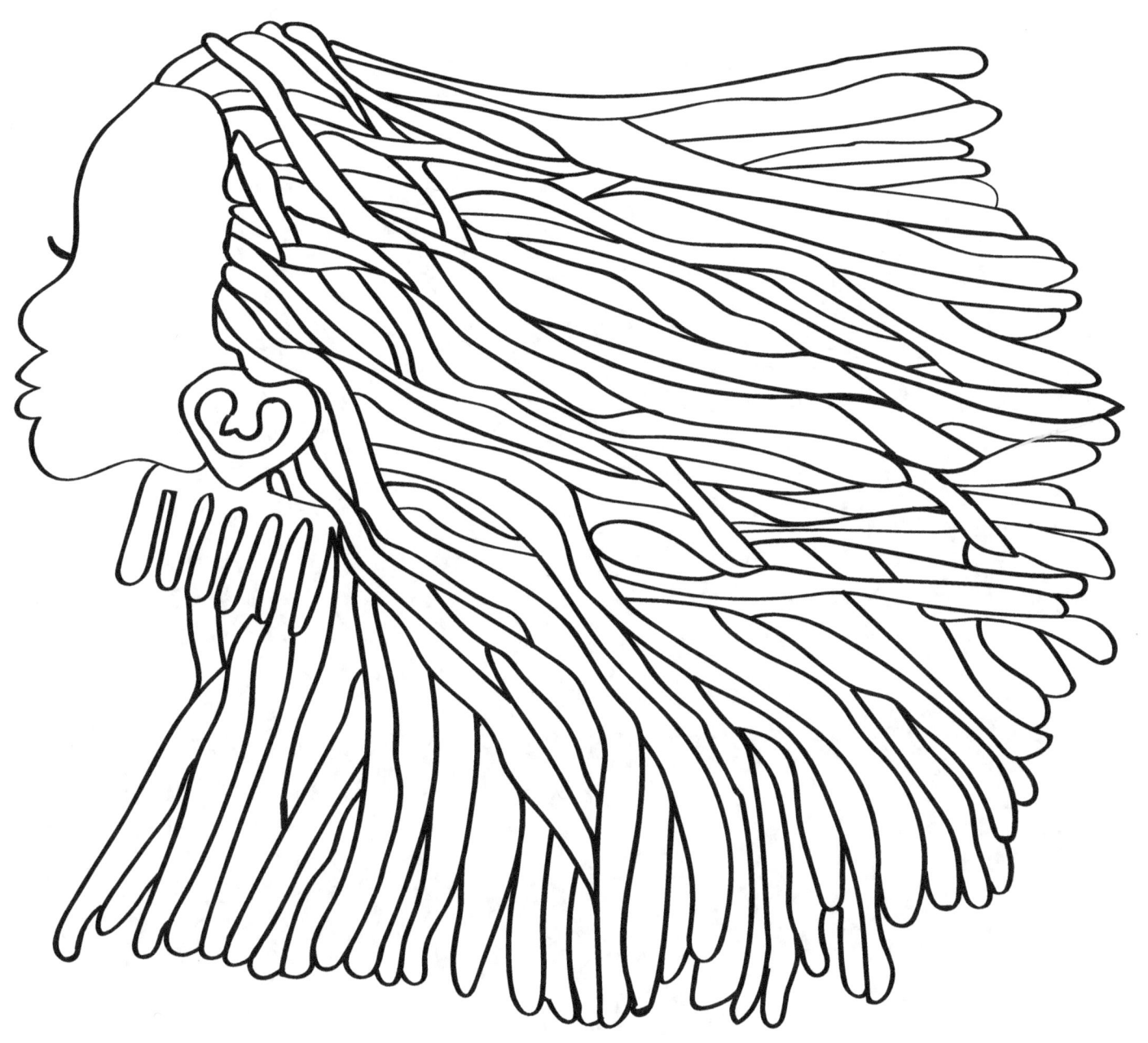

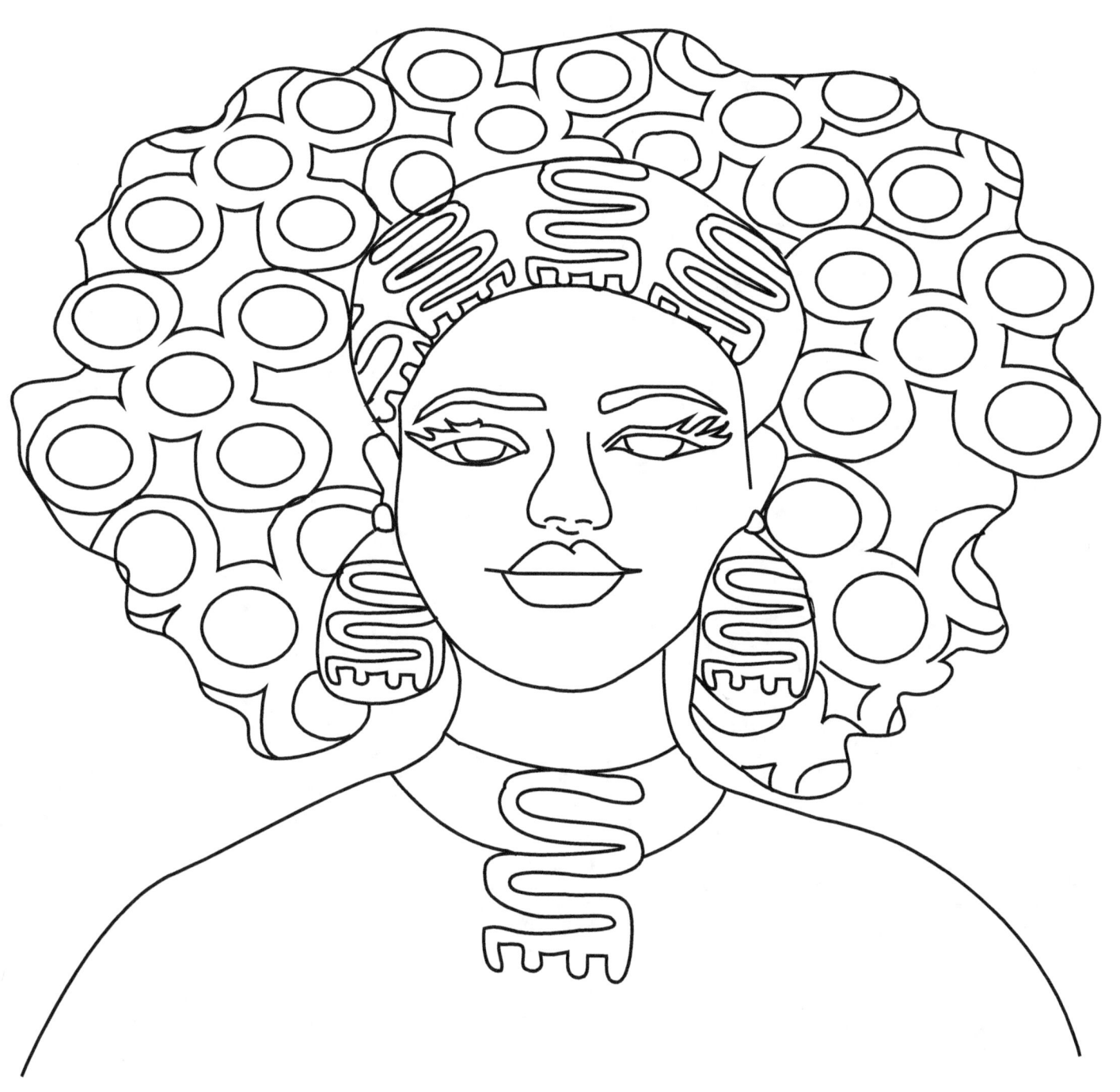

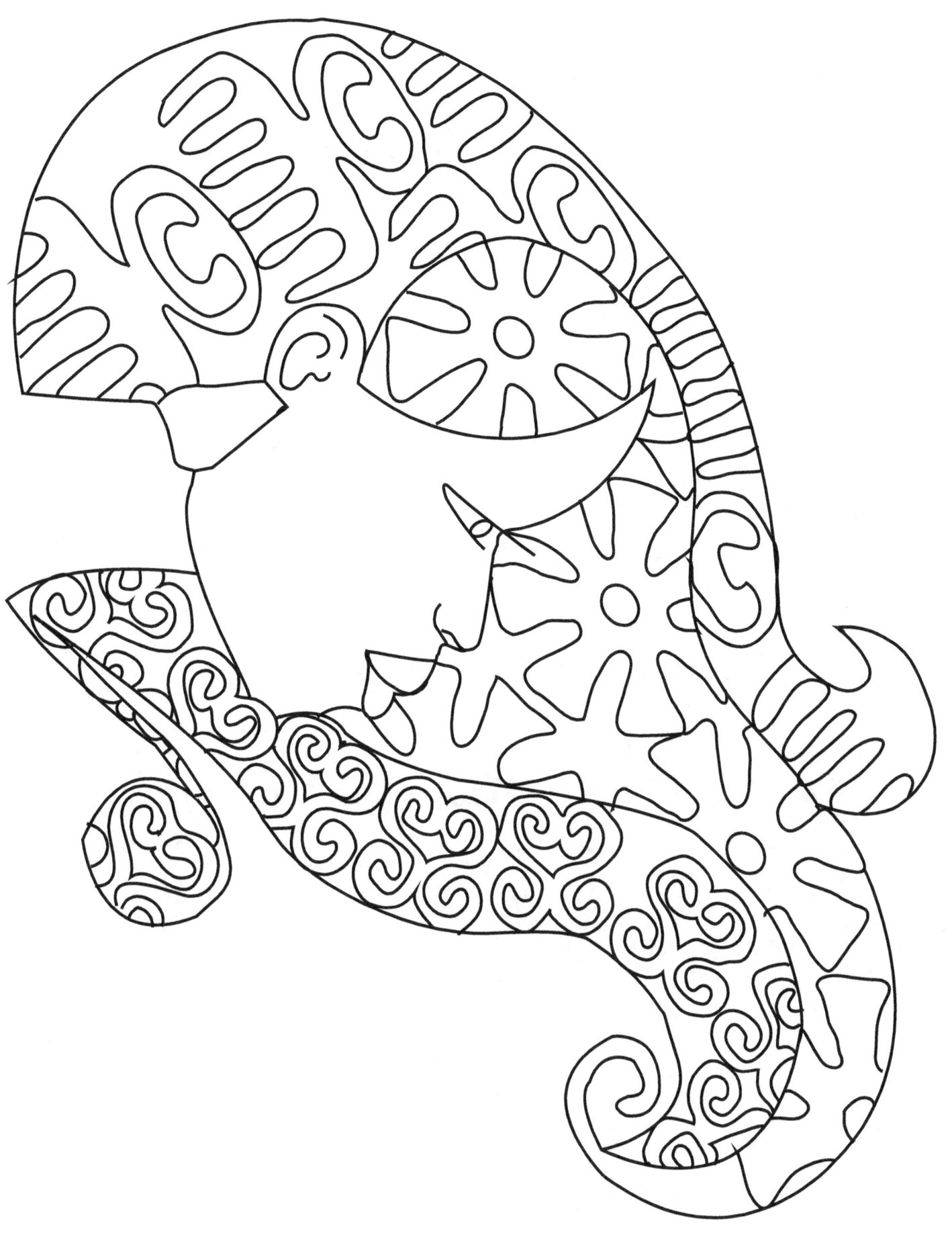

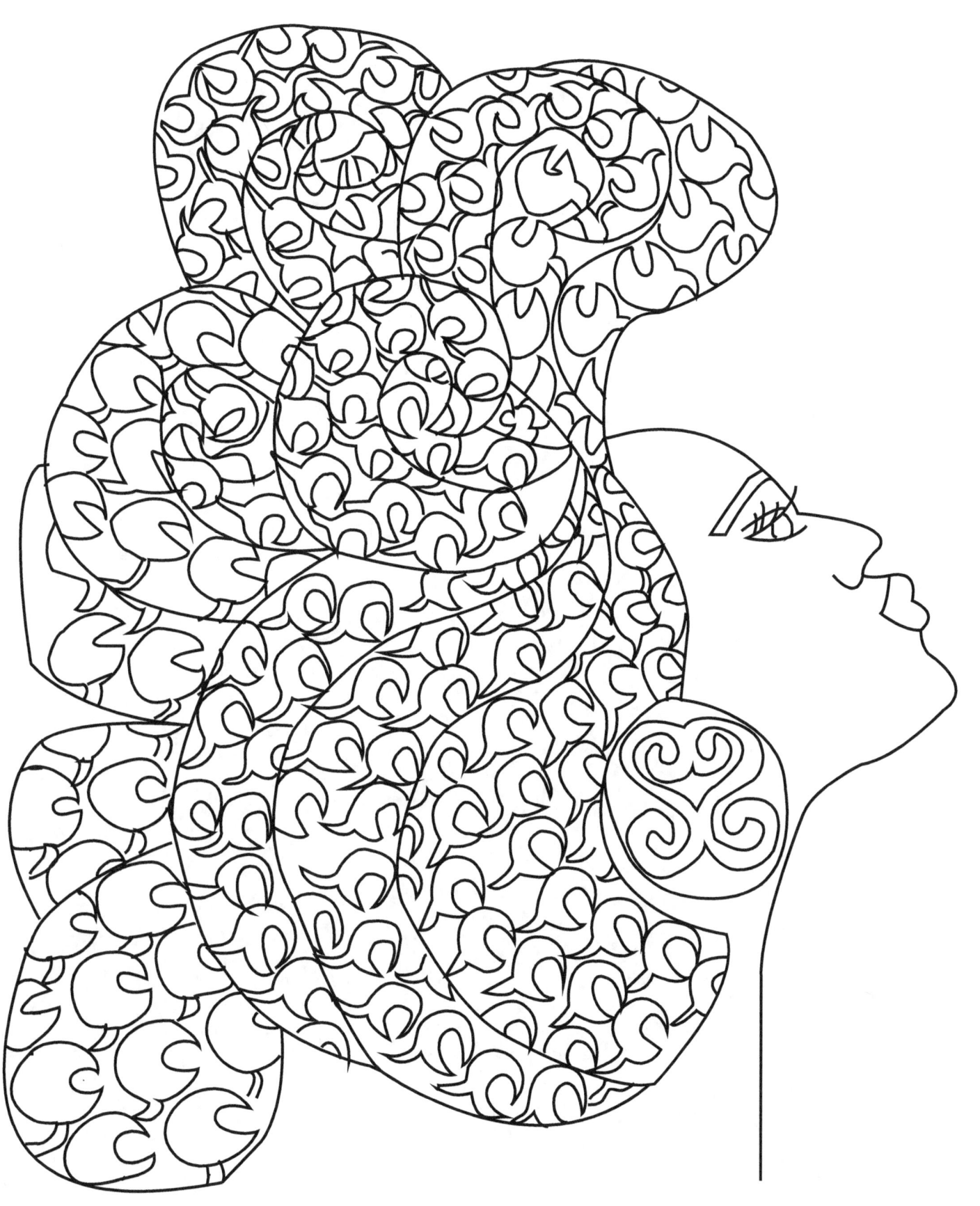

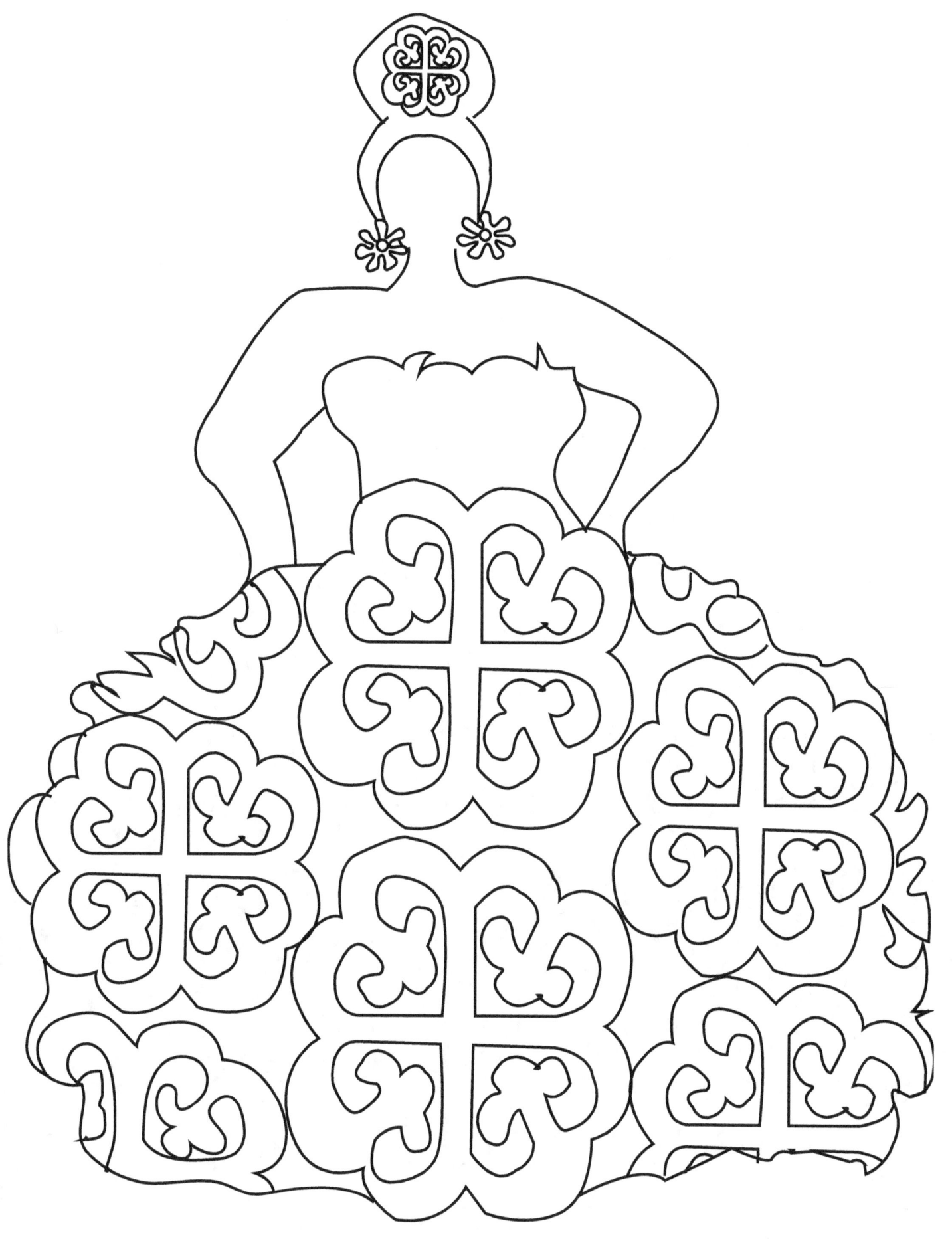

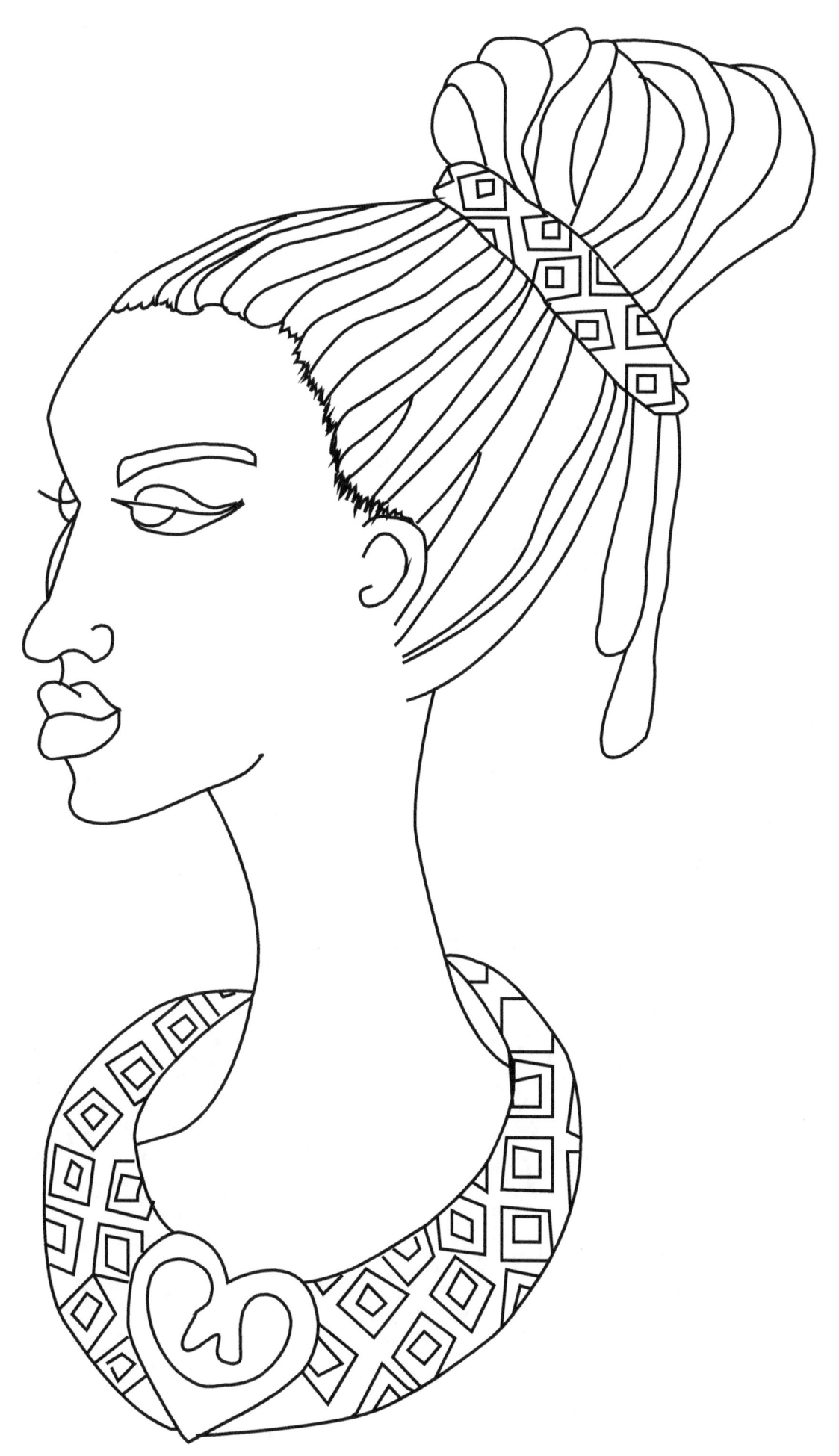

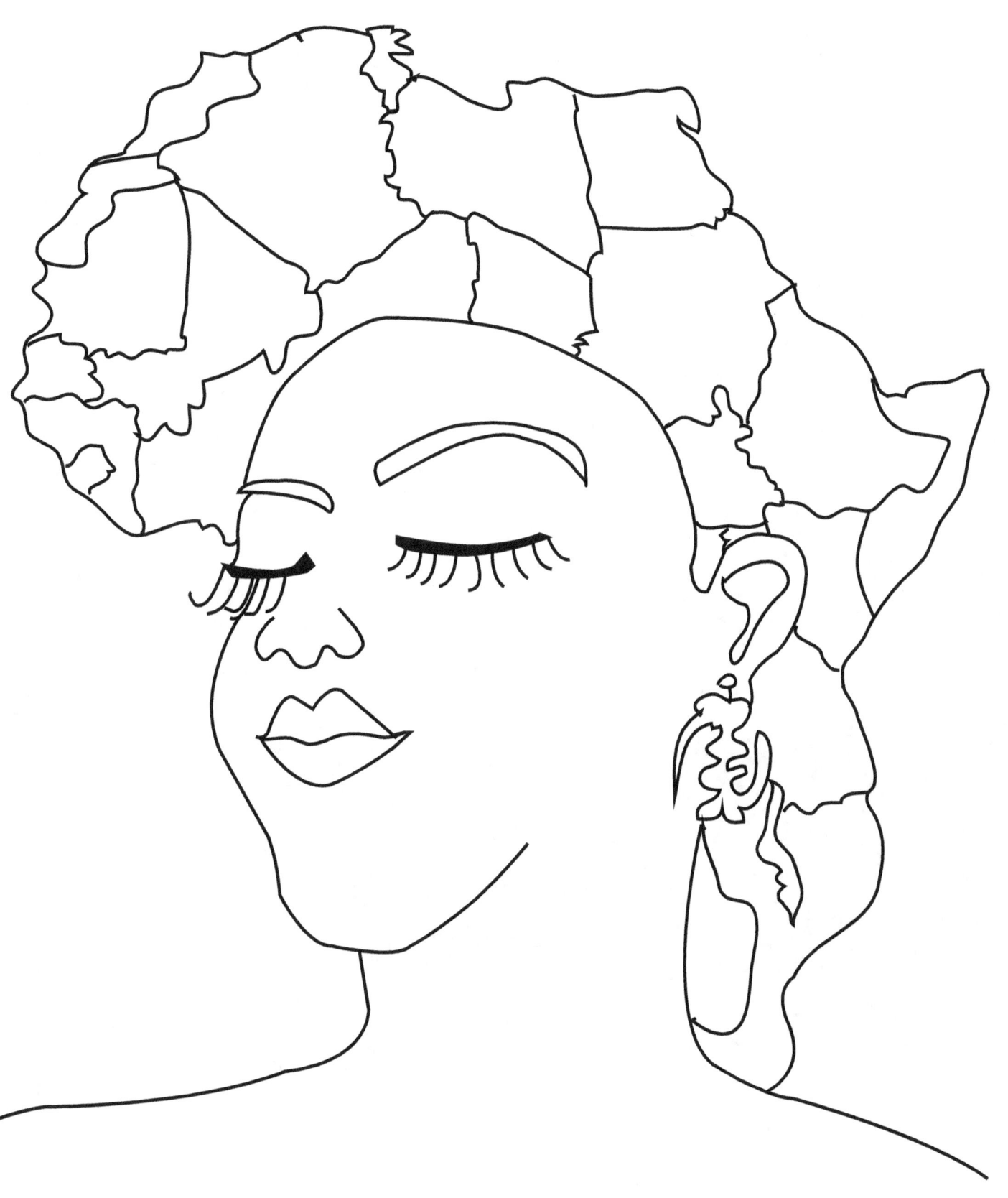

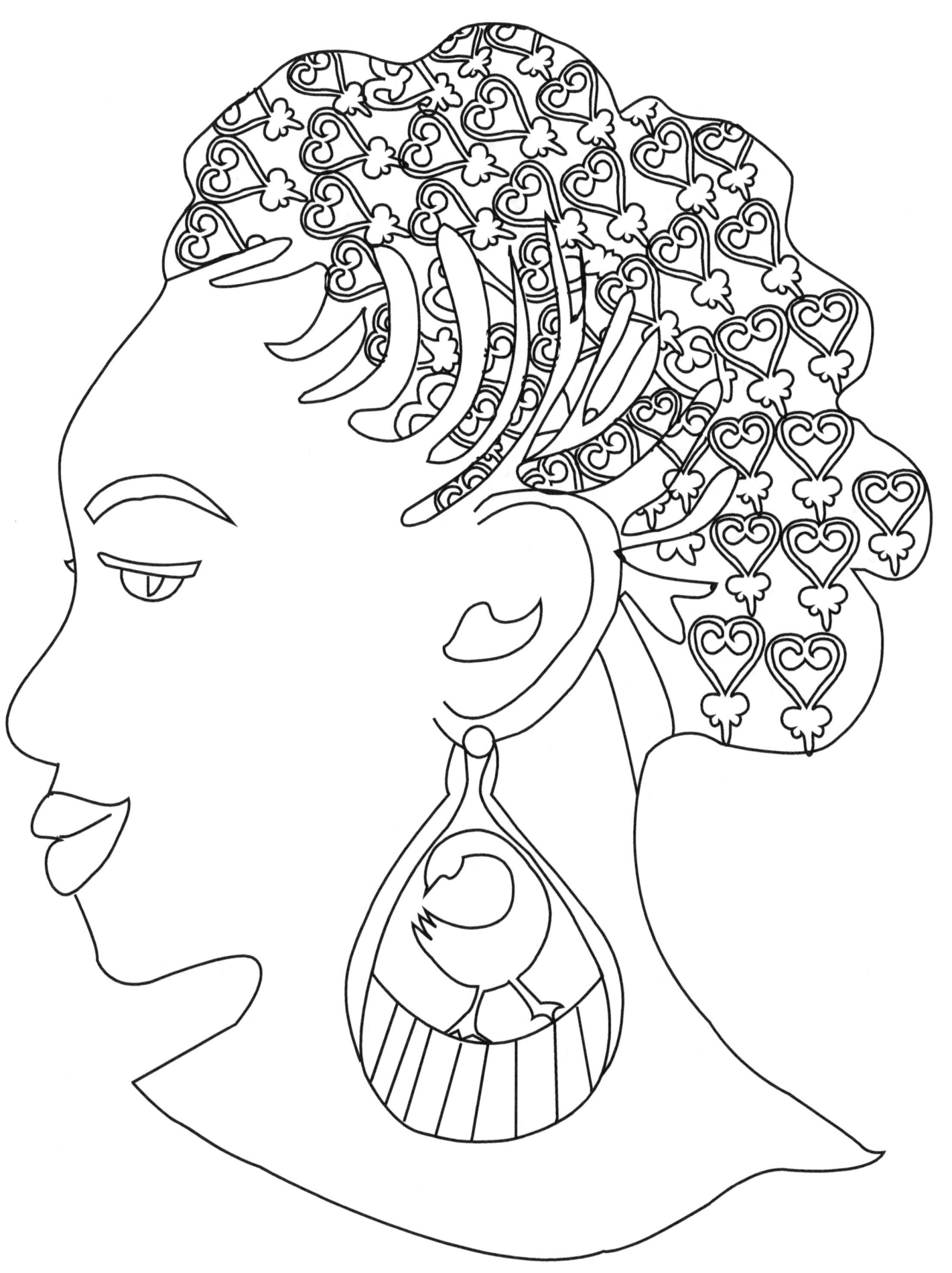

Dr. LaShawnda Lindsay-Dennis, The Crafty Ph.D.

A native of Jacksonville, Florida, LaShawnda is a formally trained African-centered educational psychologist, mental health counselor, and social scientist. In 2013, LaShawnda discovered her natural talent for "making" and merged it with her knowledge of and love for West African art and culture to launch Ananse Design Essentials. She is a self-taught craftswoman that creates each item from start to finish. Ever since then, she has constantly evolved as a maker, artist, entrepreneur, scholar, craftswoman, and activist.

LaShawnda served as a college professor for over seven years and is currently a research scientist at the Wellesley Centers for Women. In 2015, she was recognized by The Augusta Metro Chamber of Commerce, in partnership with Augusta Magazine, as one of Augusta's ten most outstanding young professionals. She is also the founder of Black Girls Matter, a social media campaign to bring awareness to issues that Black girls face in global society.

With deep devotion, LaShawnda has vigorously accepted the call to enhance the well-being and lives of Black girls globally. Her wide array of research over the past decade has created a platform that sheds light on the social determinants, racial injustices, and cultural biases that burden the progression and viability of Black women. This devotion emerges in her scholarly work as well as her craftswomanship.

To learn more about LaShawnda and her work, visit AnanseDesignEssentials.com